Geometrix Eleven

LOUISE ATHERTON

ISBN-13: 978-1546988465
ISBN-10: 1546988467

Testing – Use this page to test your writing implements and color palettes.

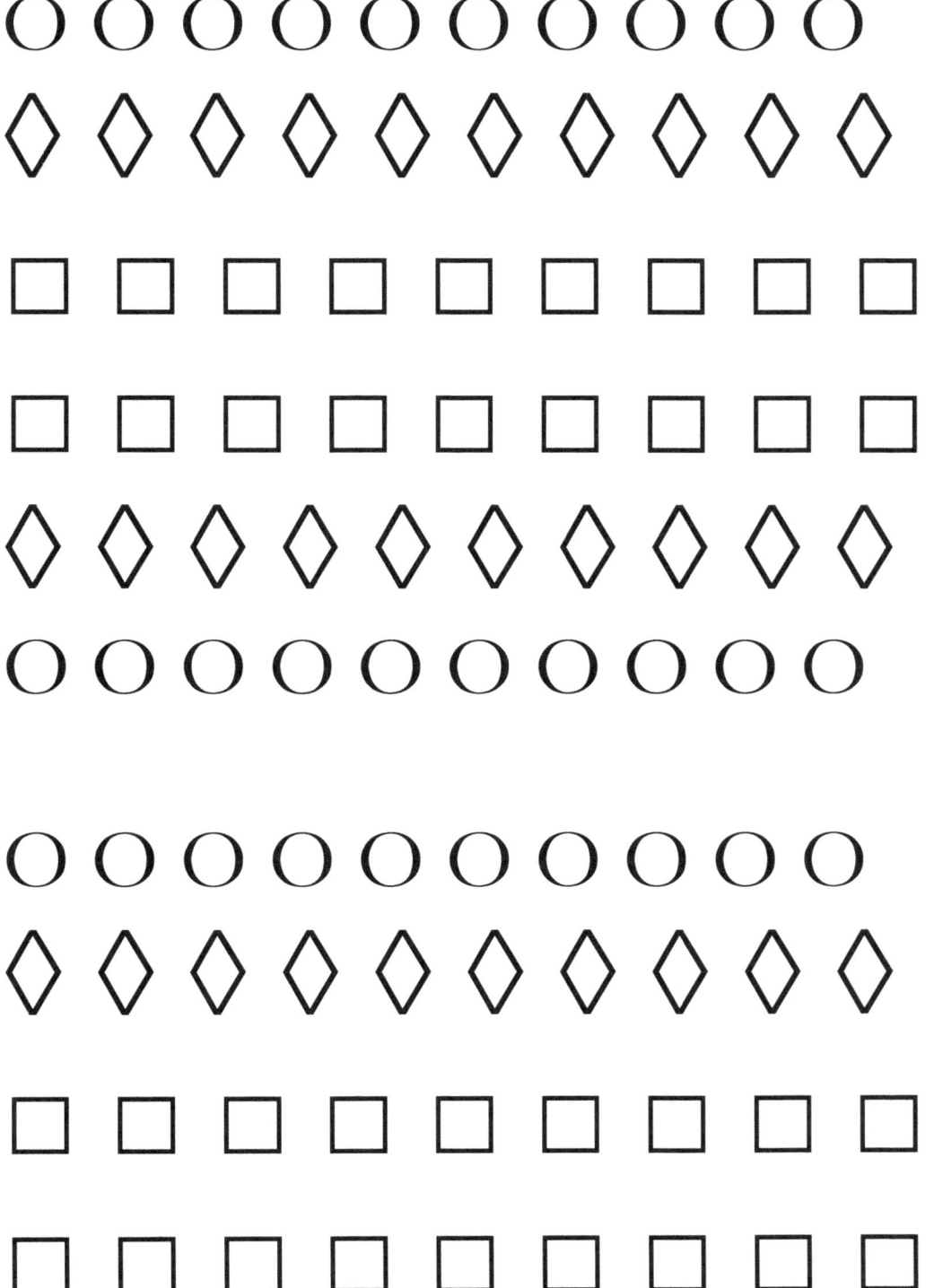

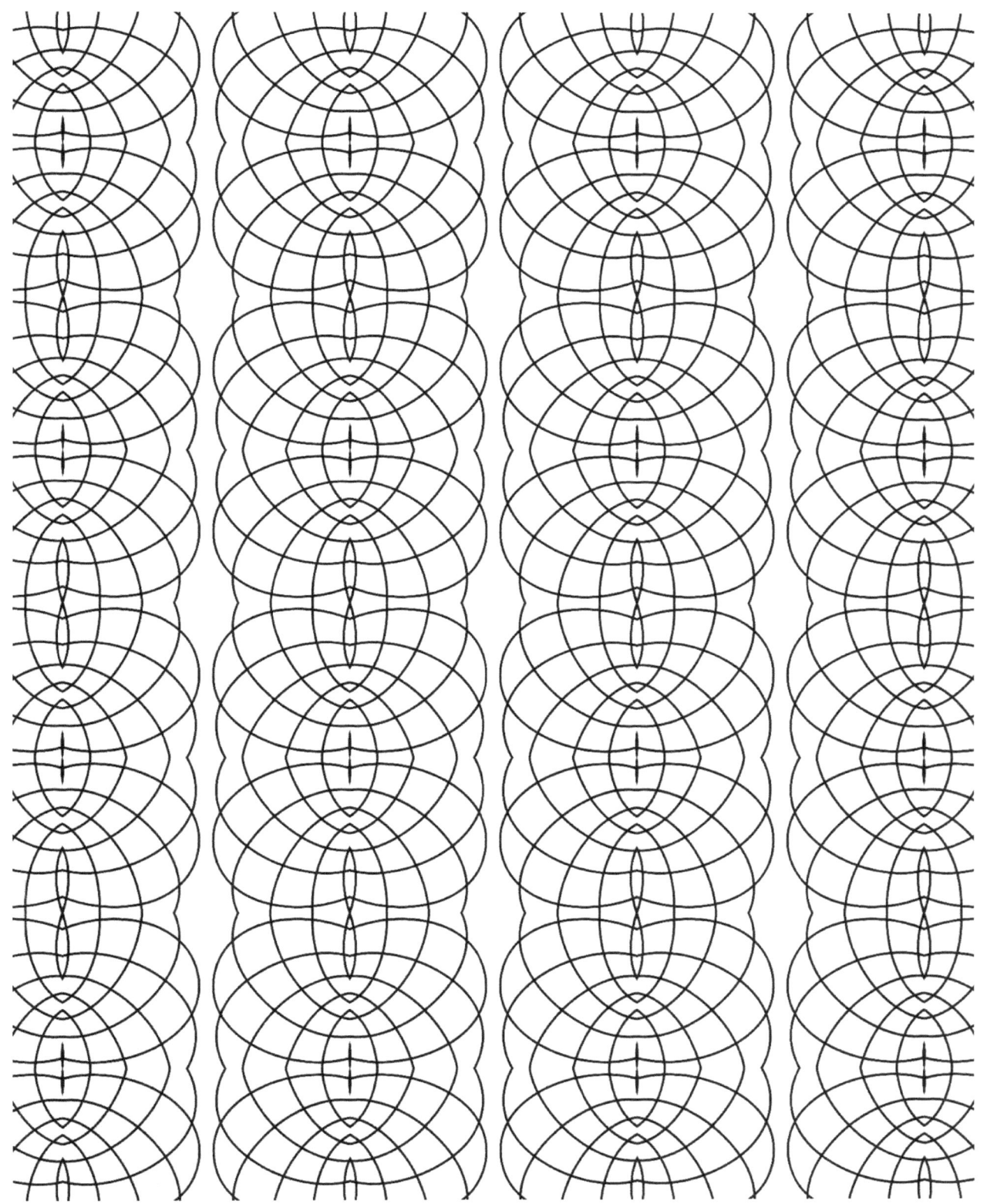

LOUISE ATHERTON

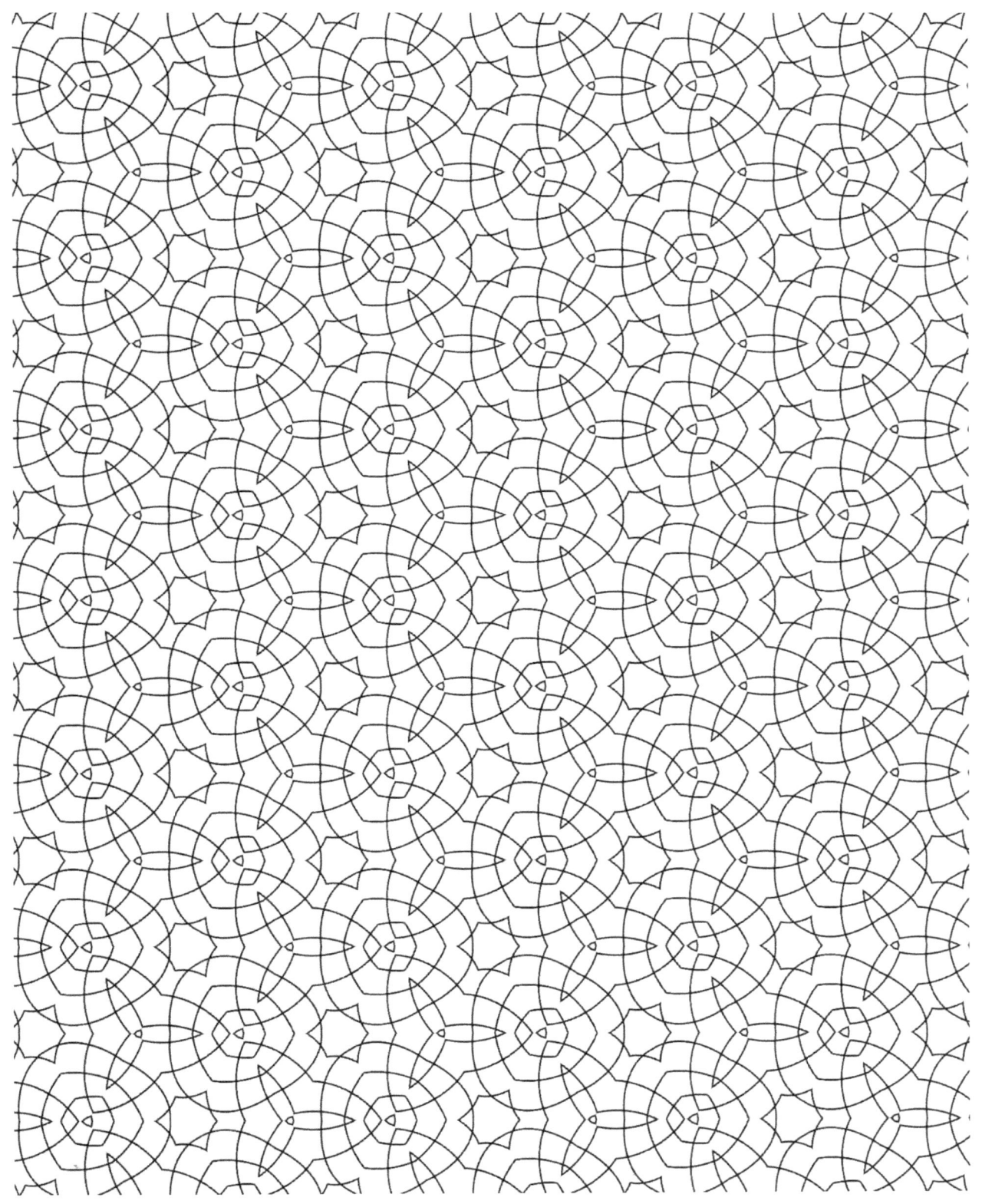

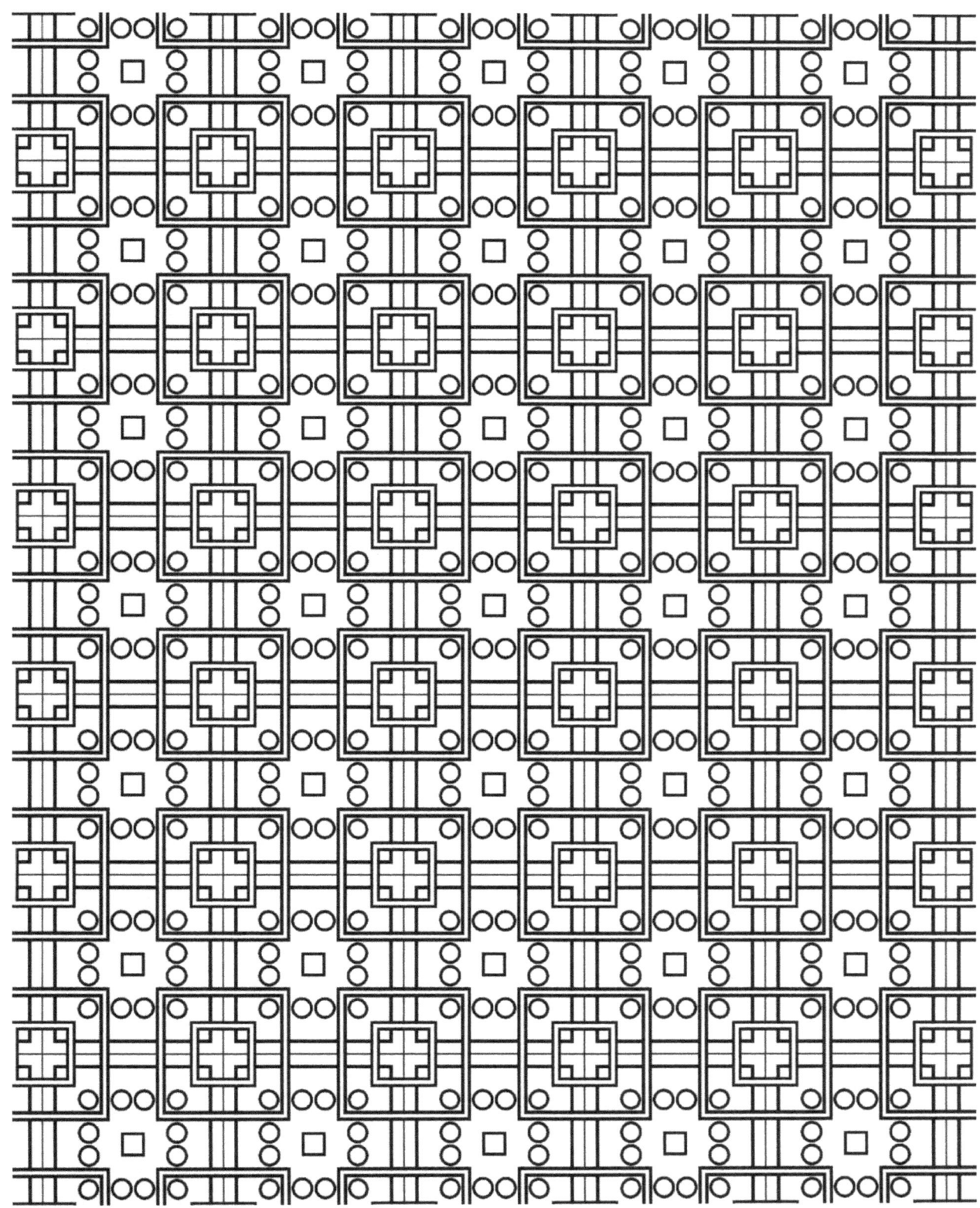

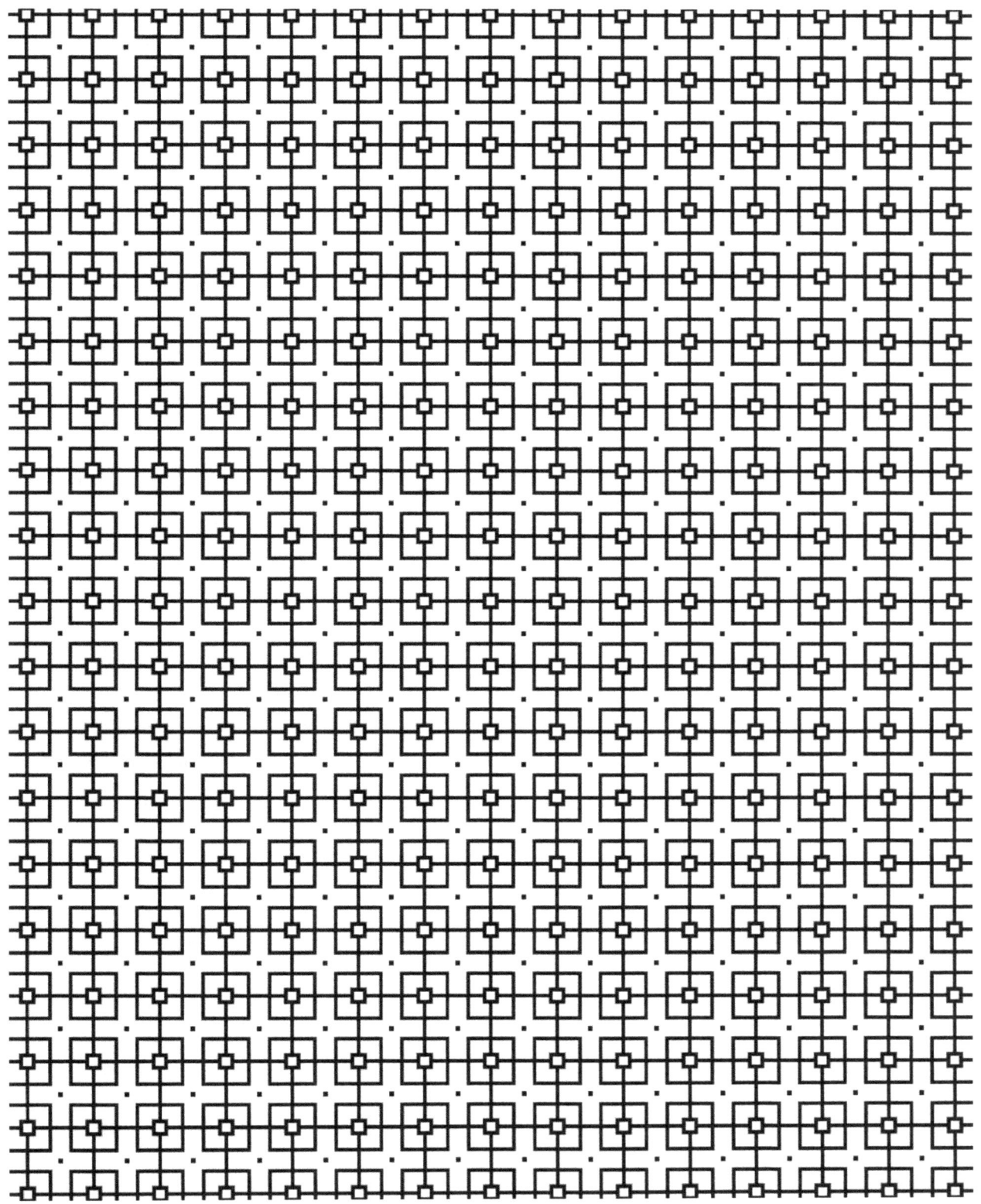

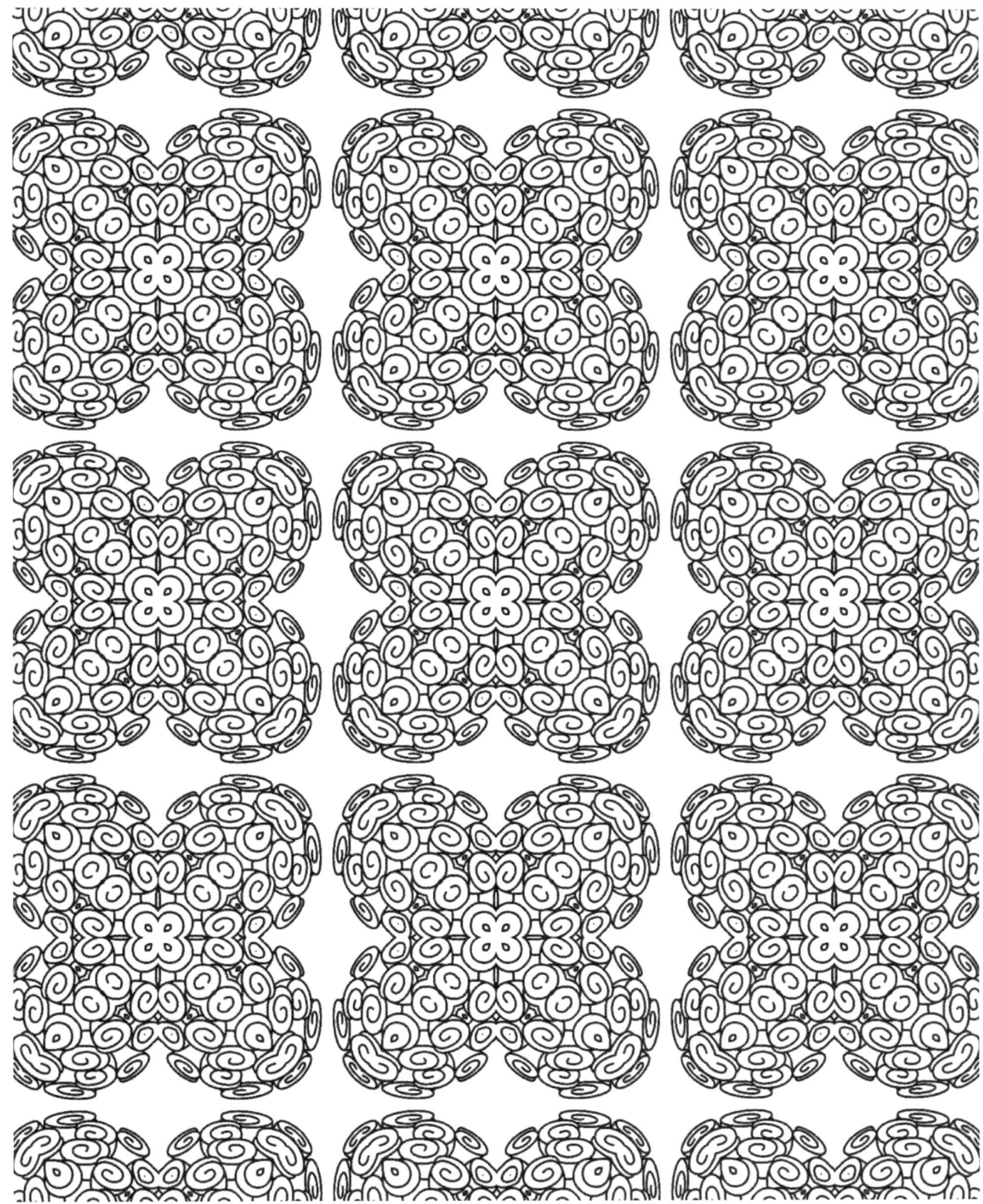

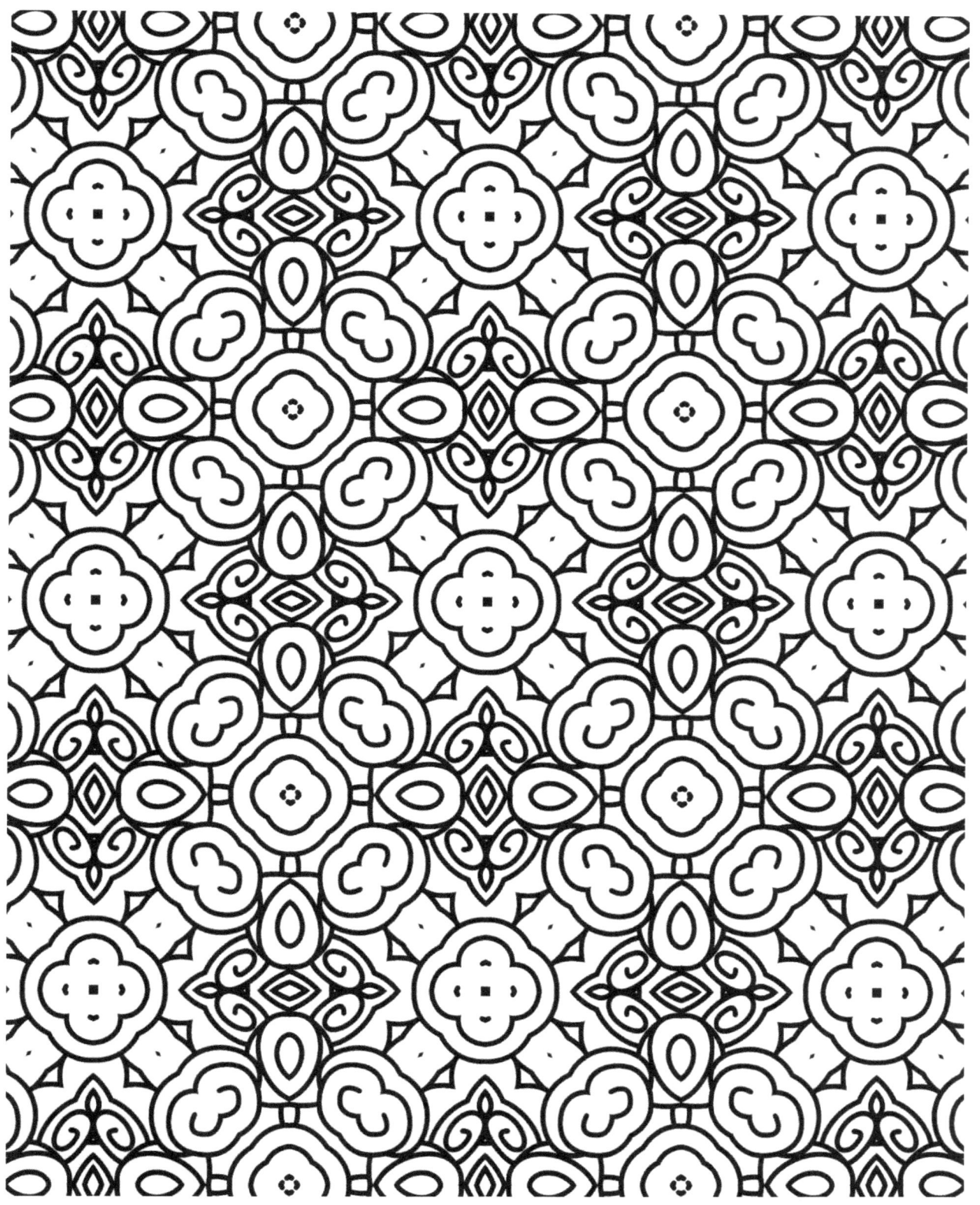

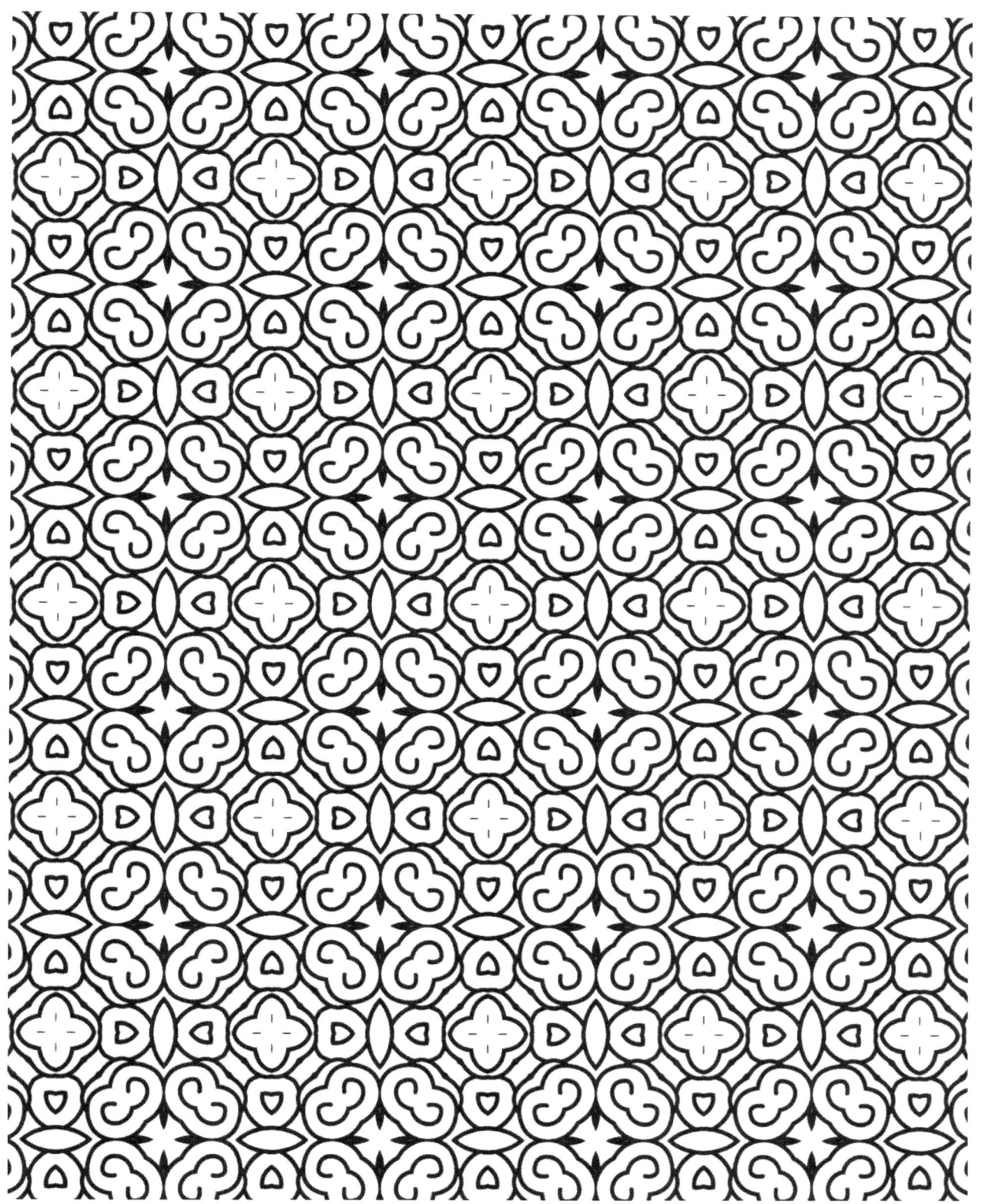

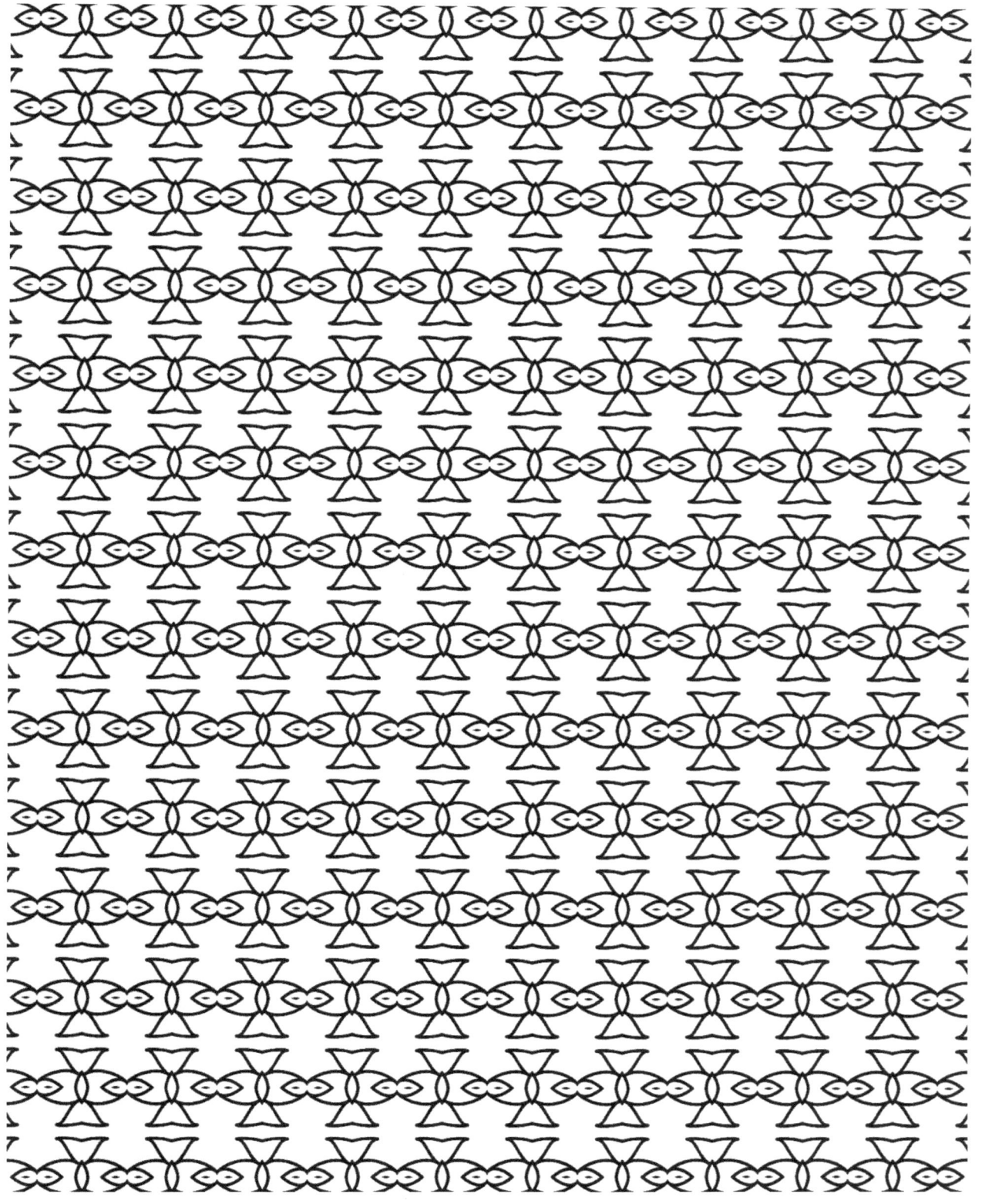

LOUISE ATHERTON

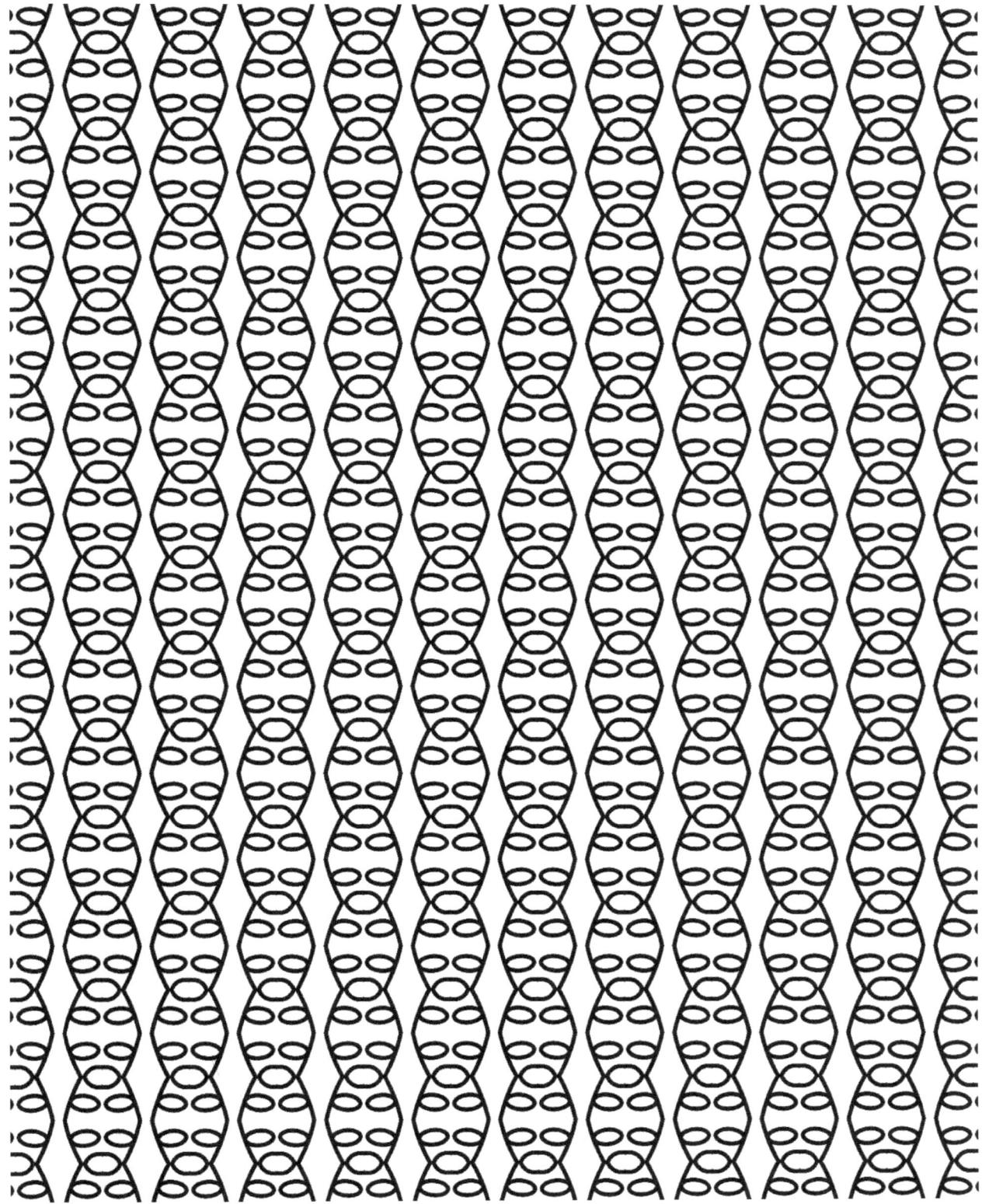

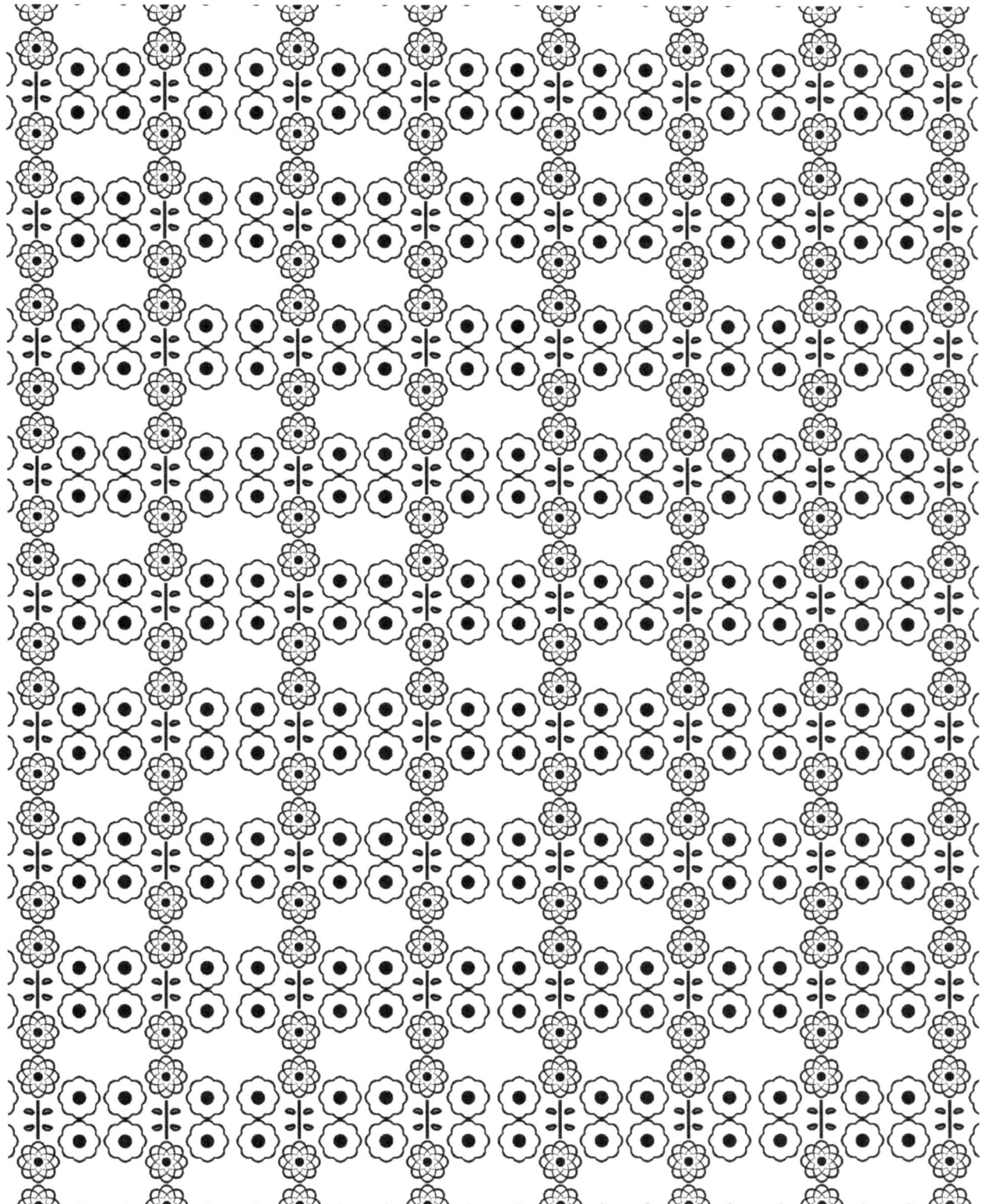

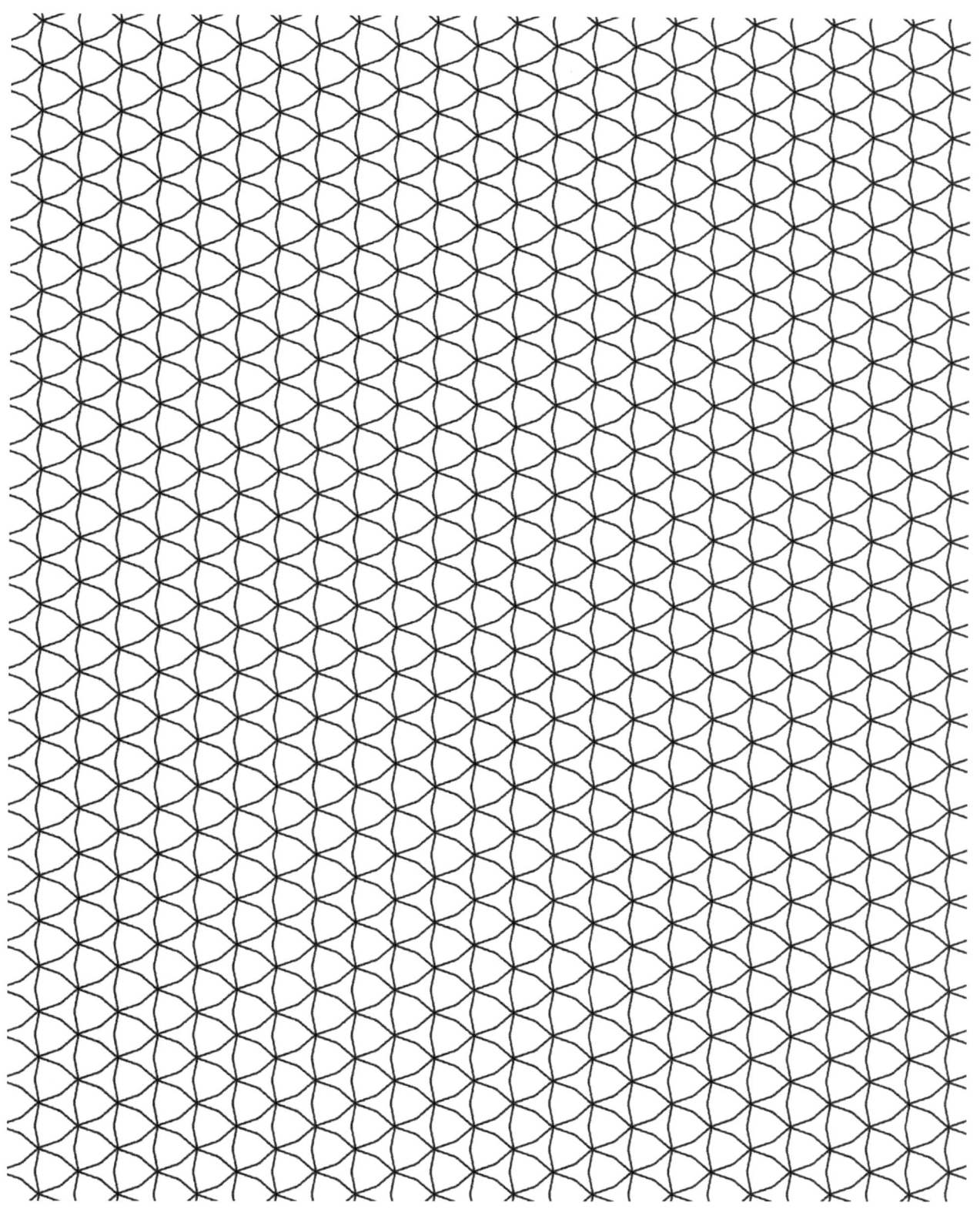

LOUISE ATHERTON

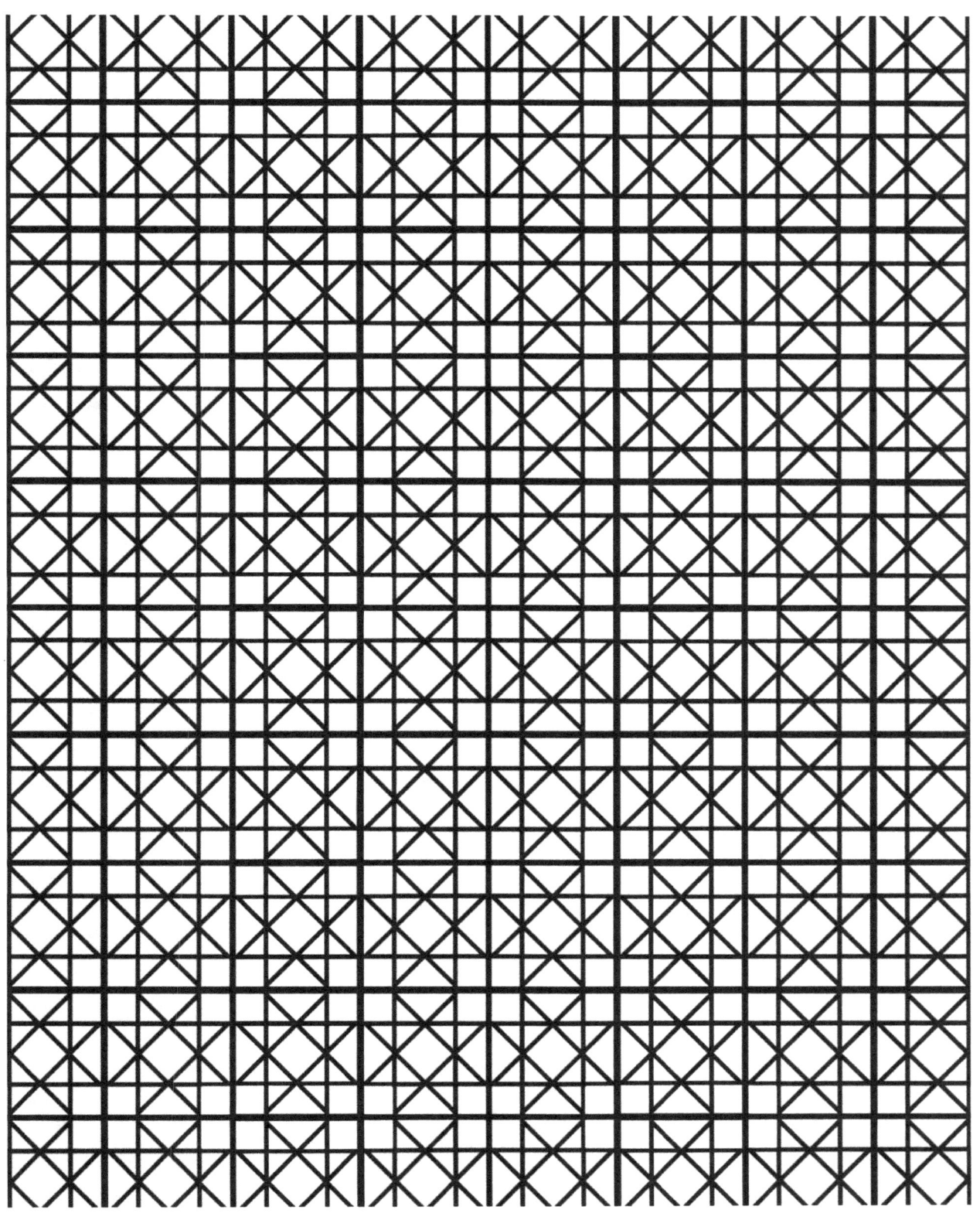

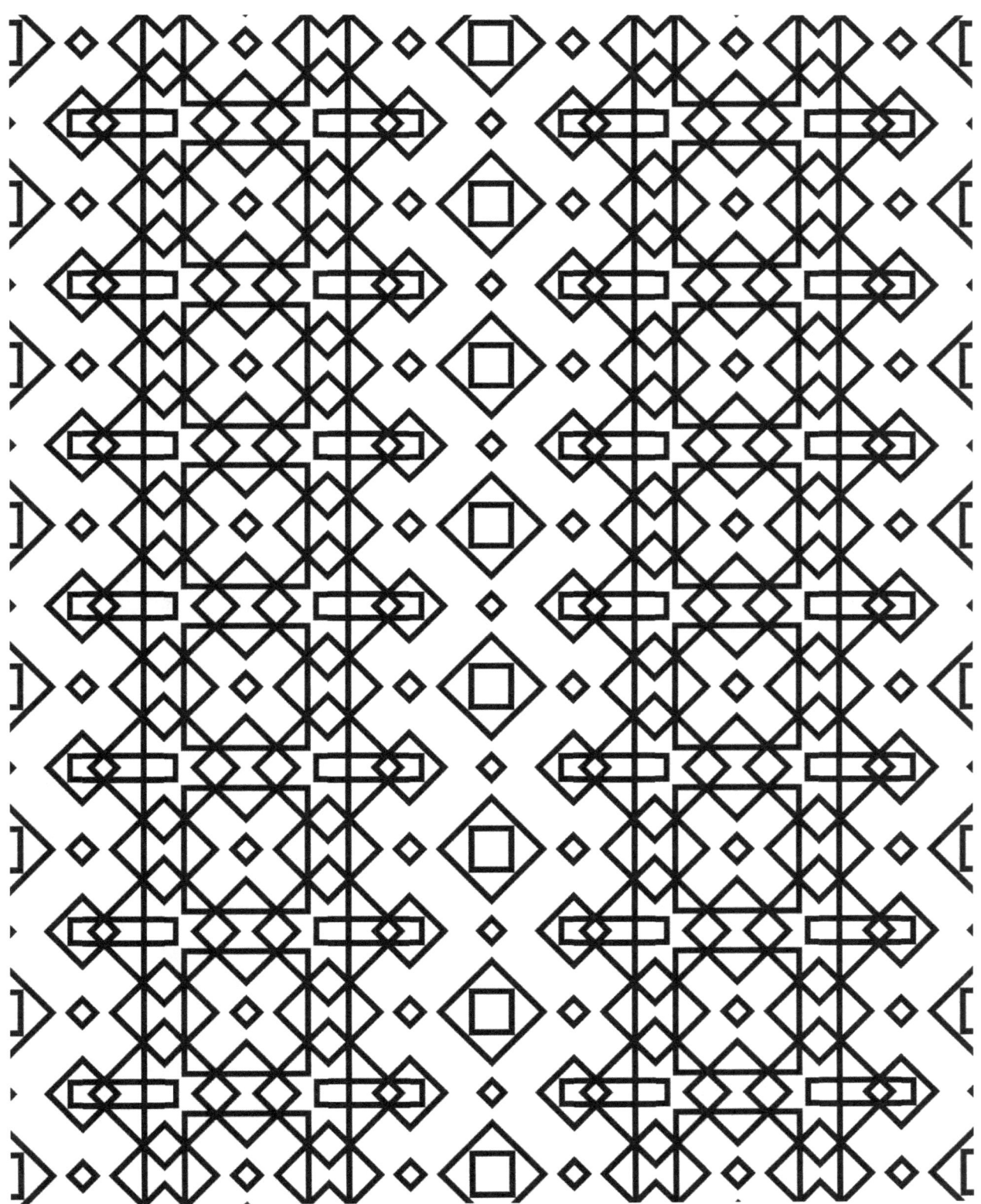

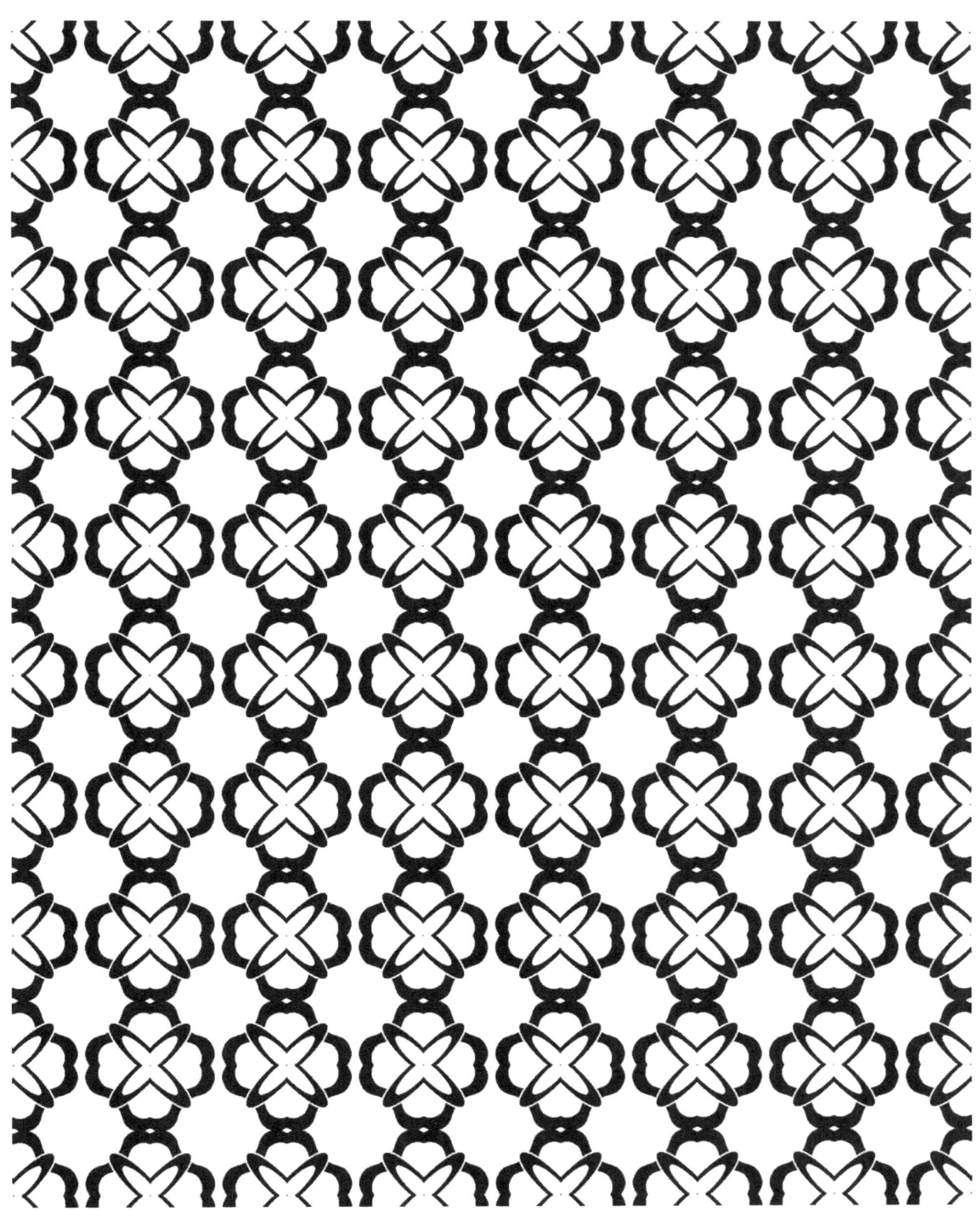

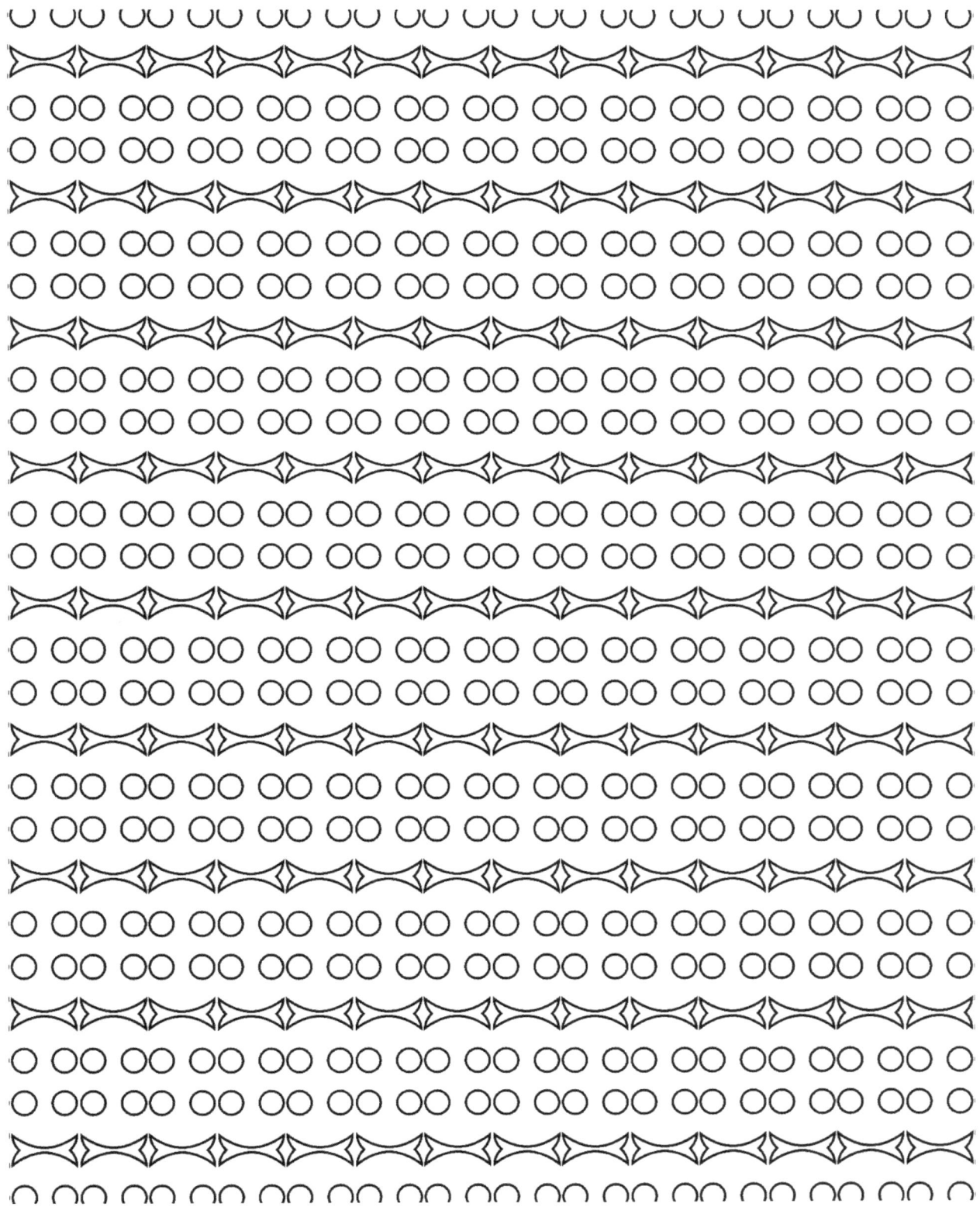

LOUISE ATHERTON

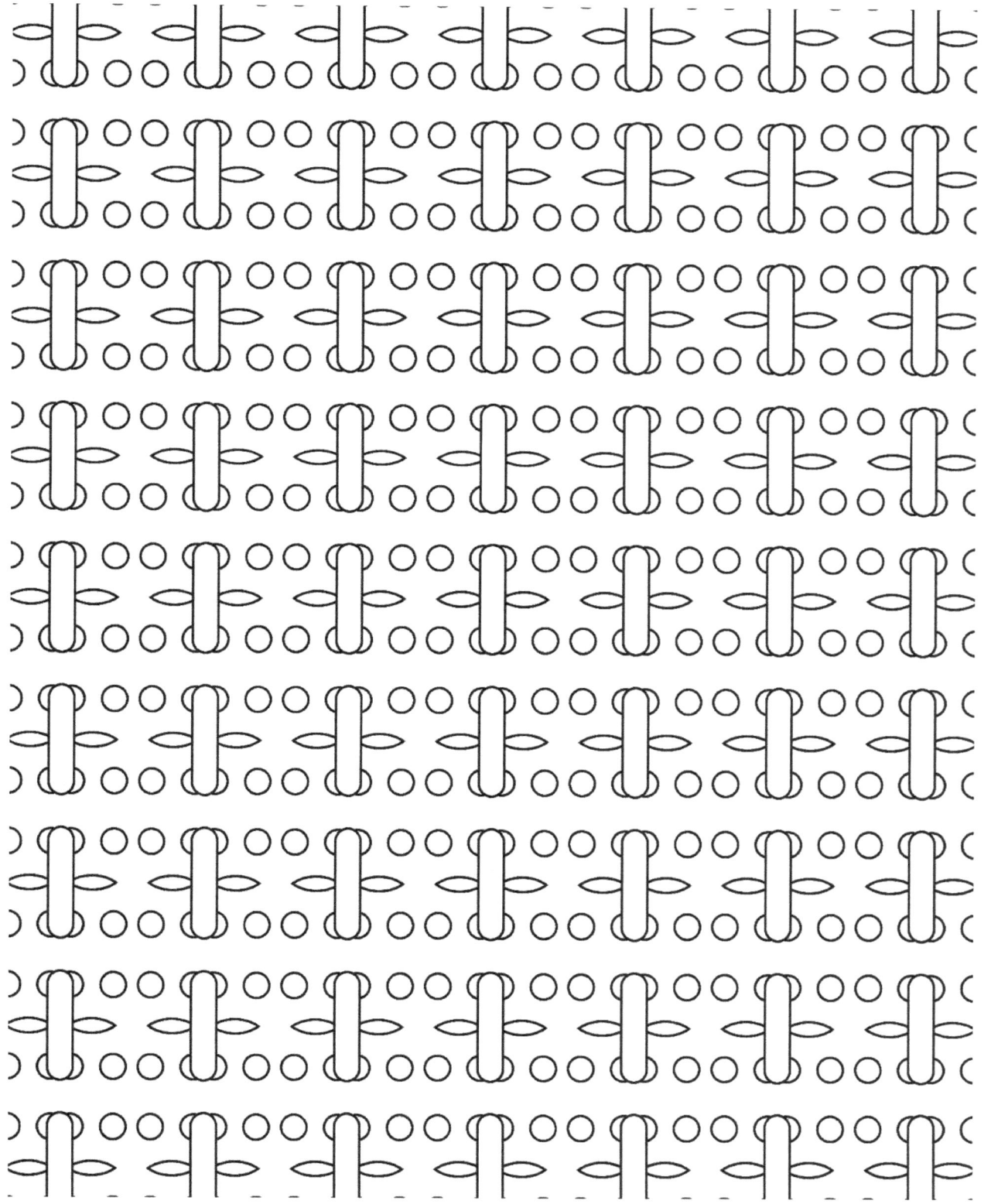

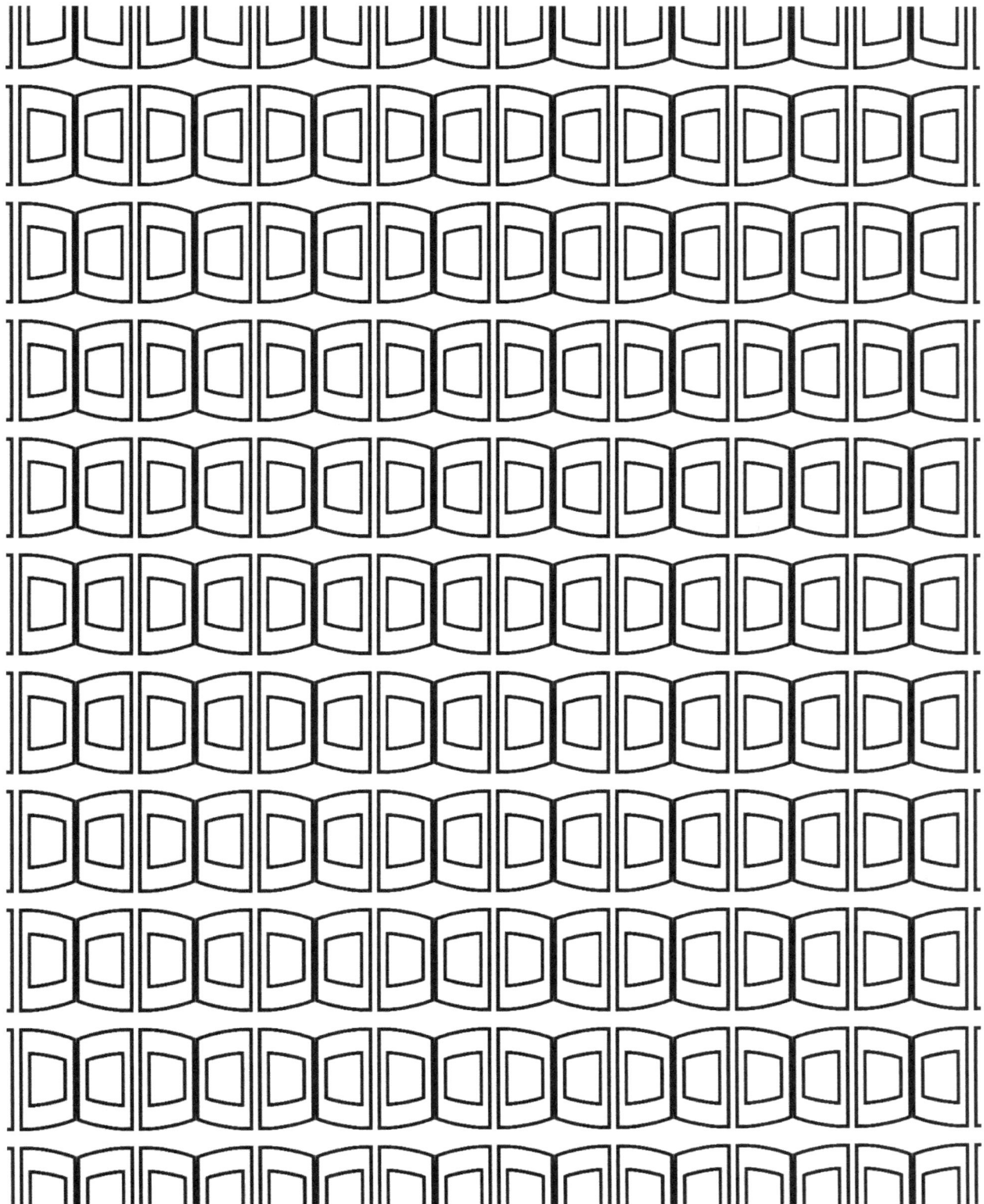

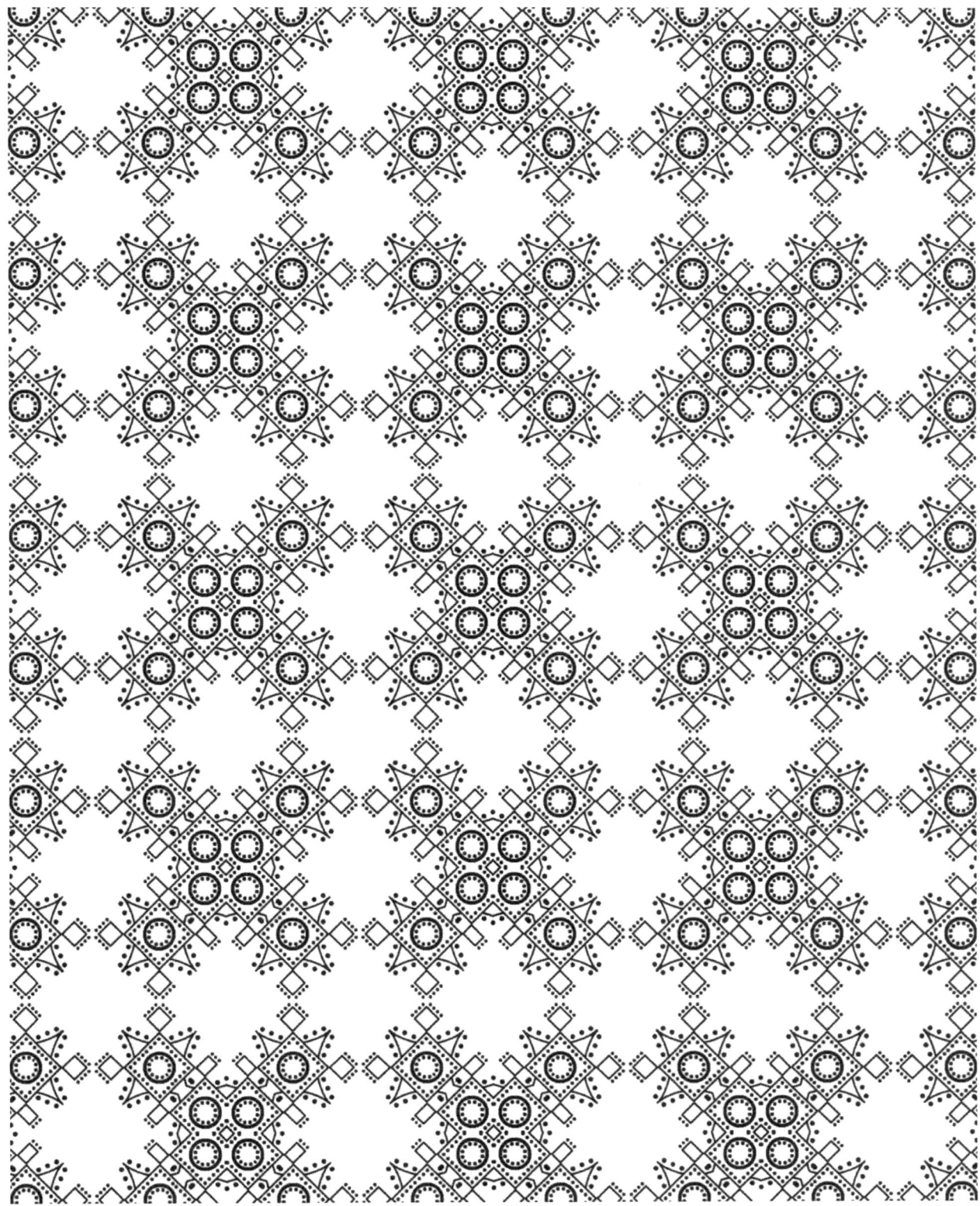

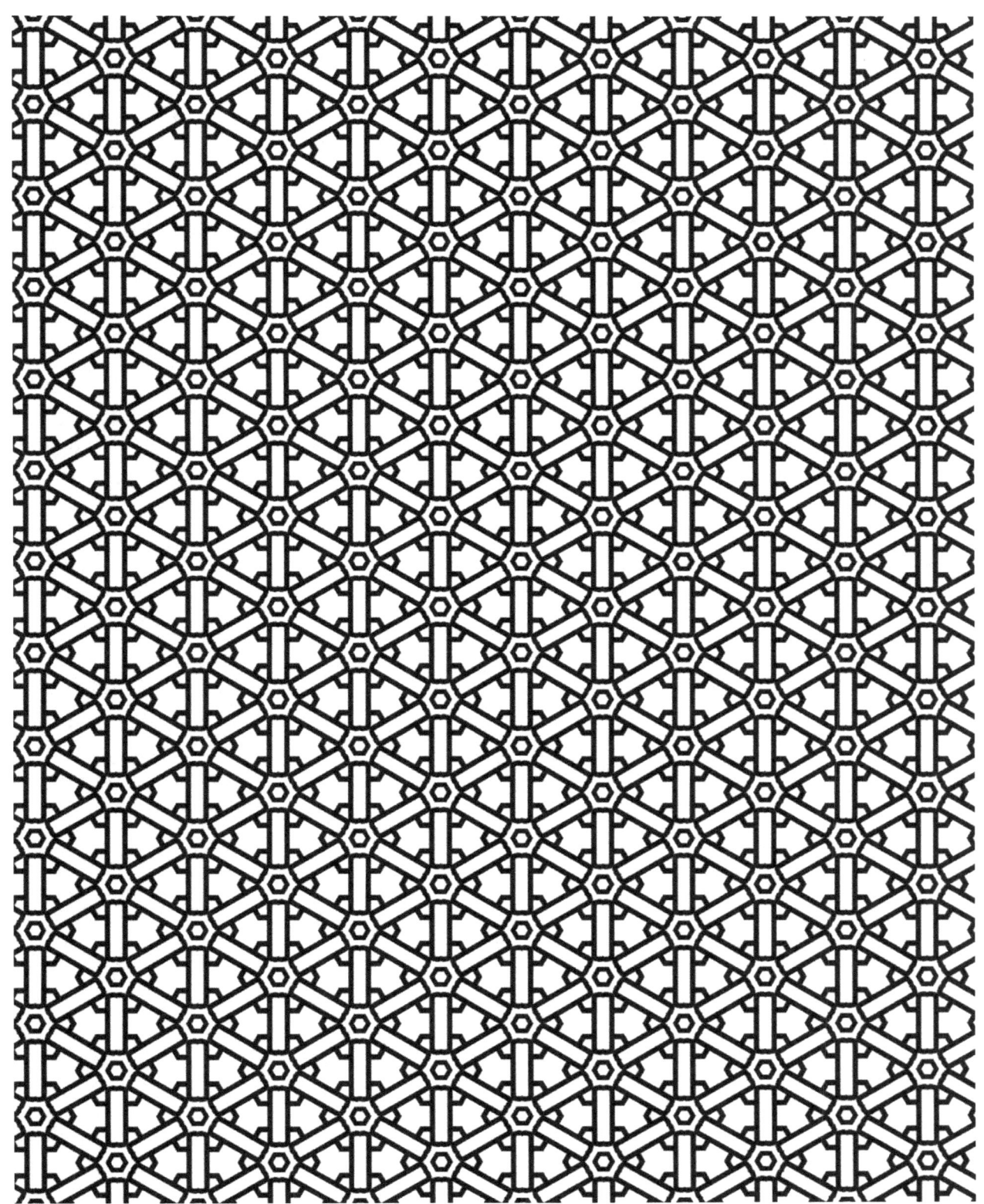

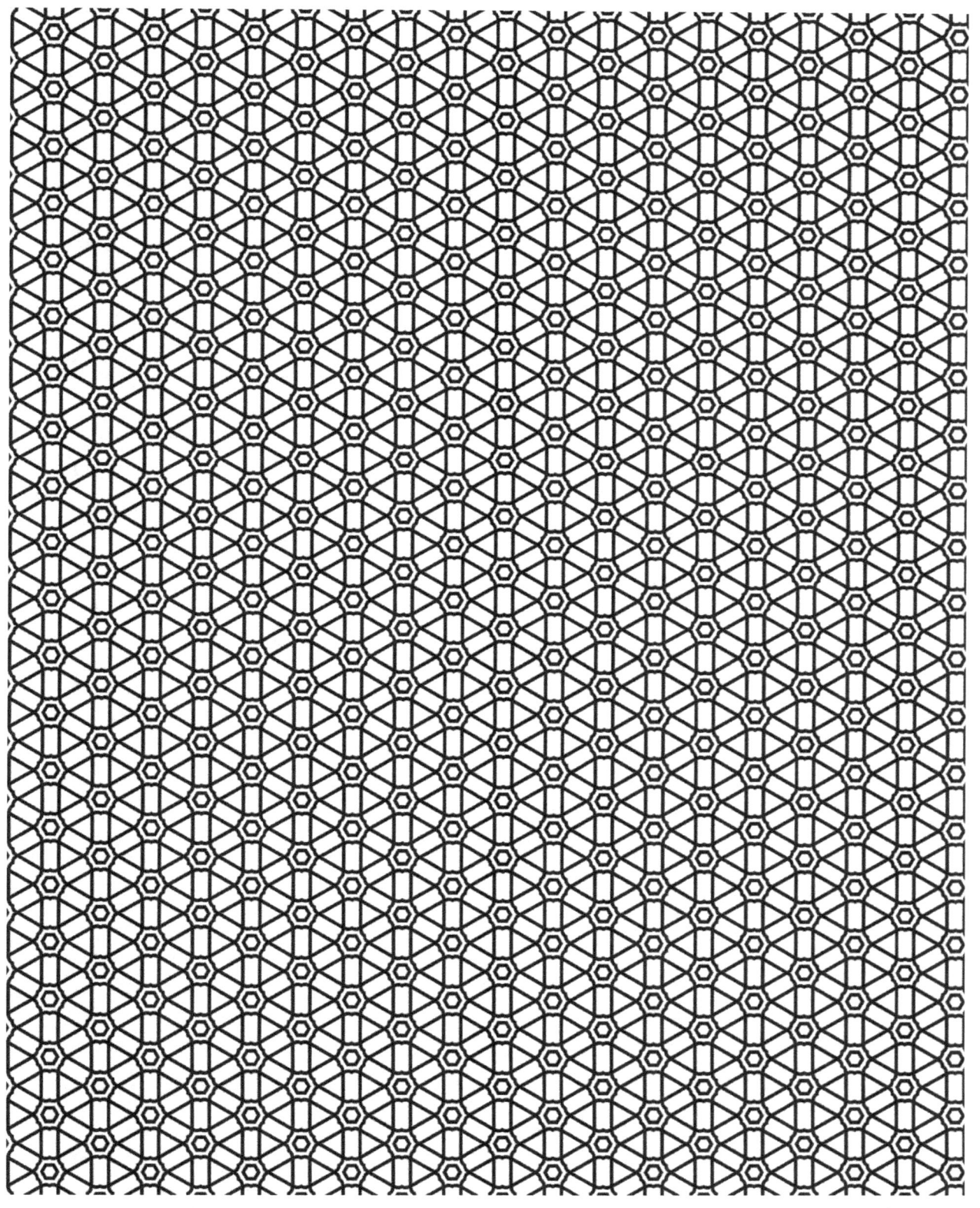

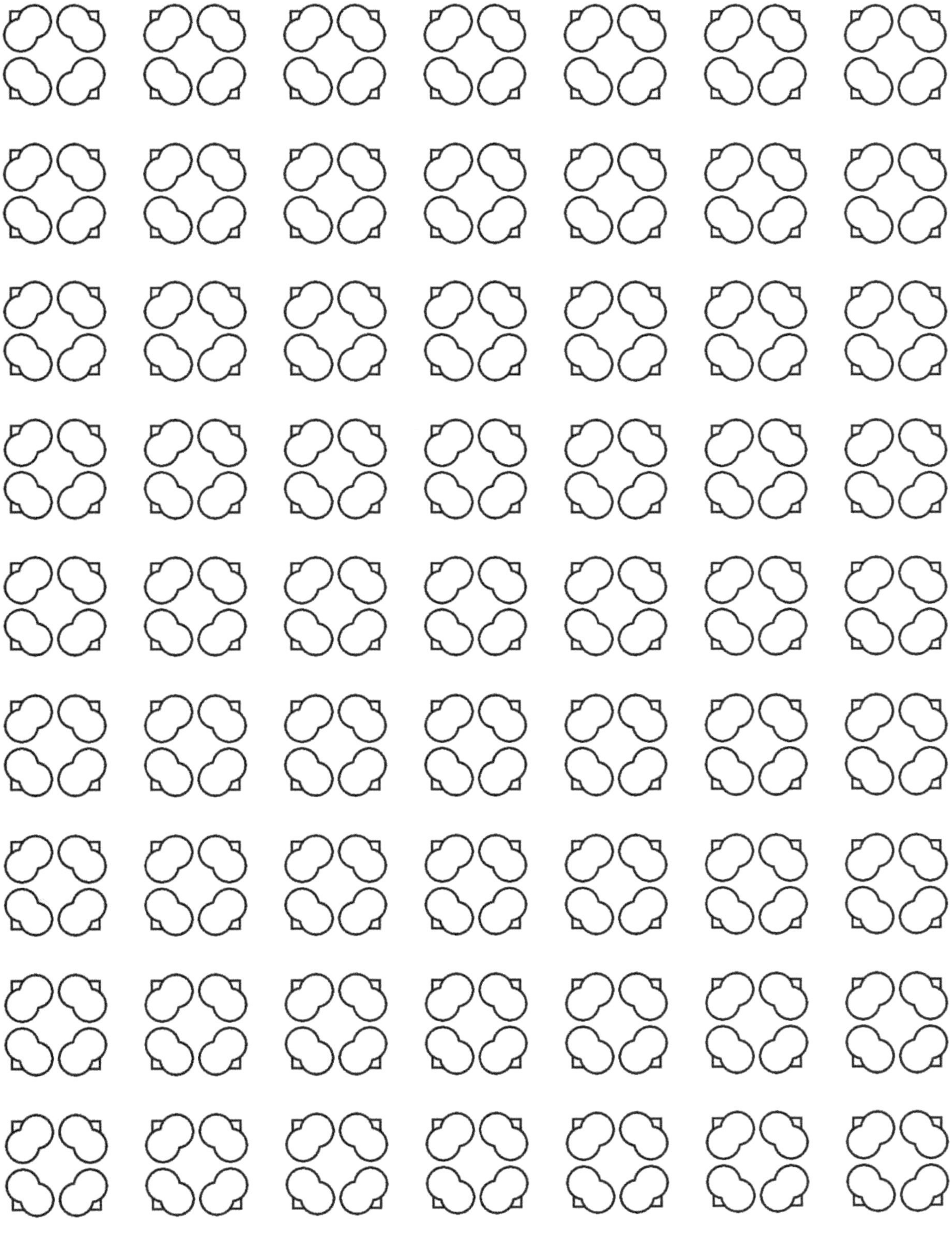

LOUISE ATHERTON

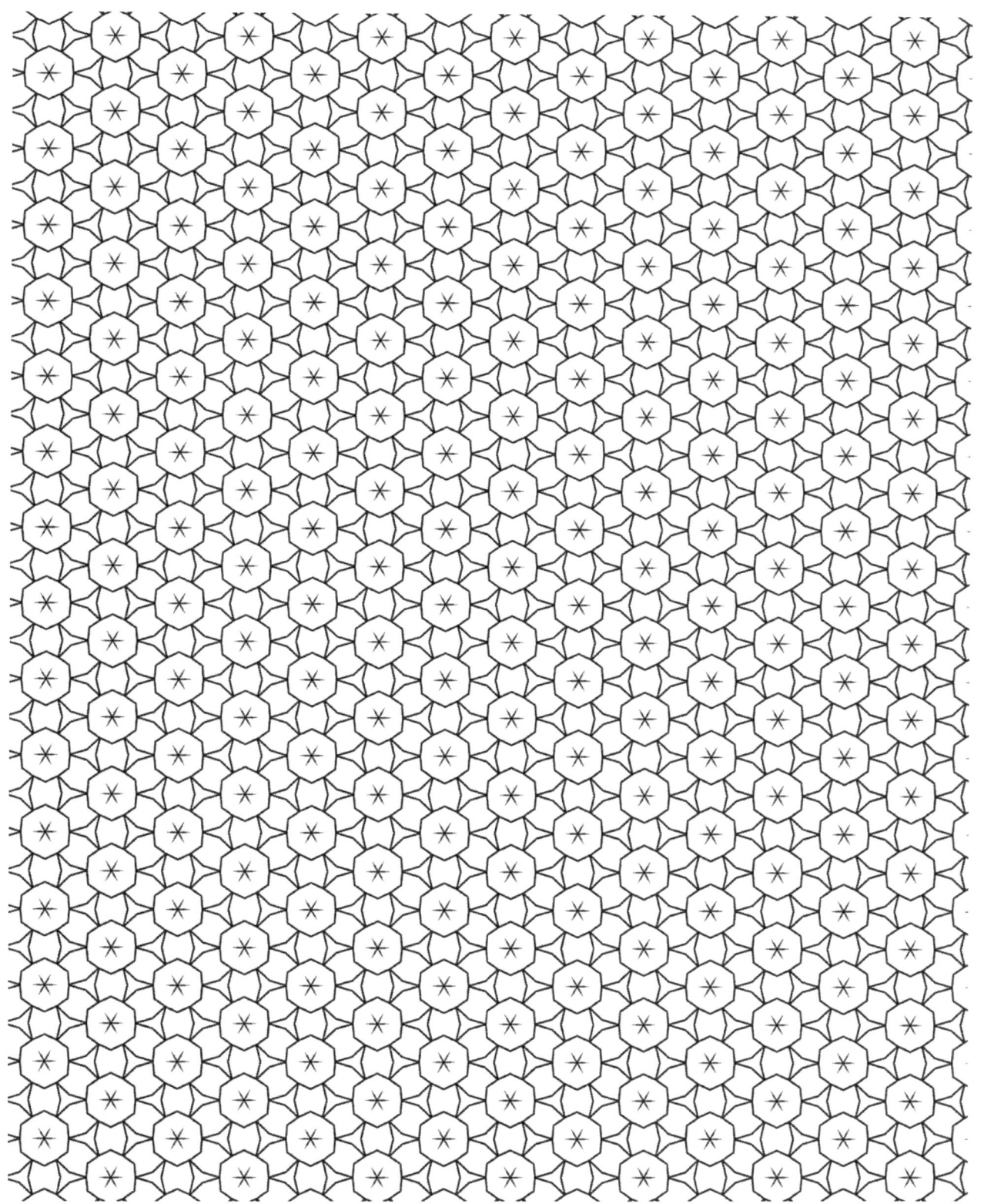

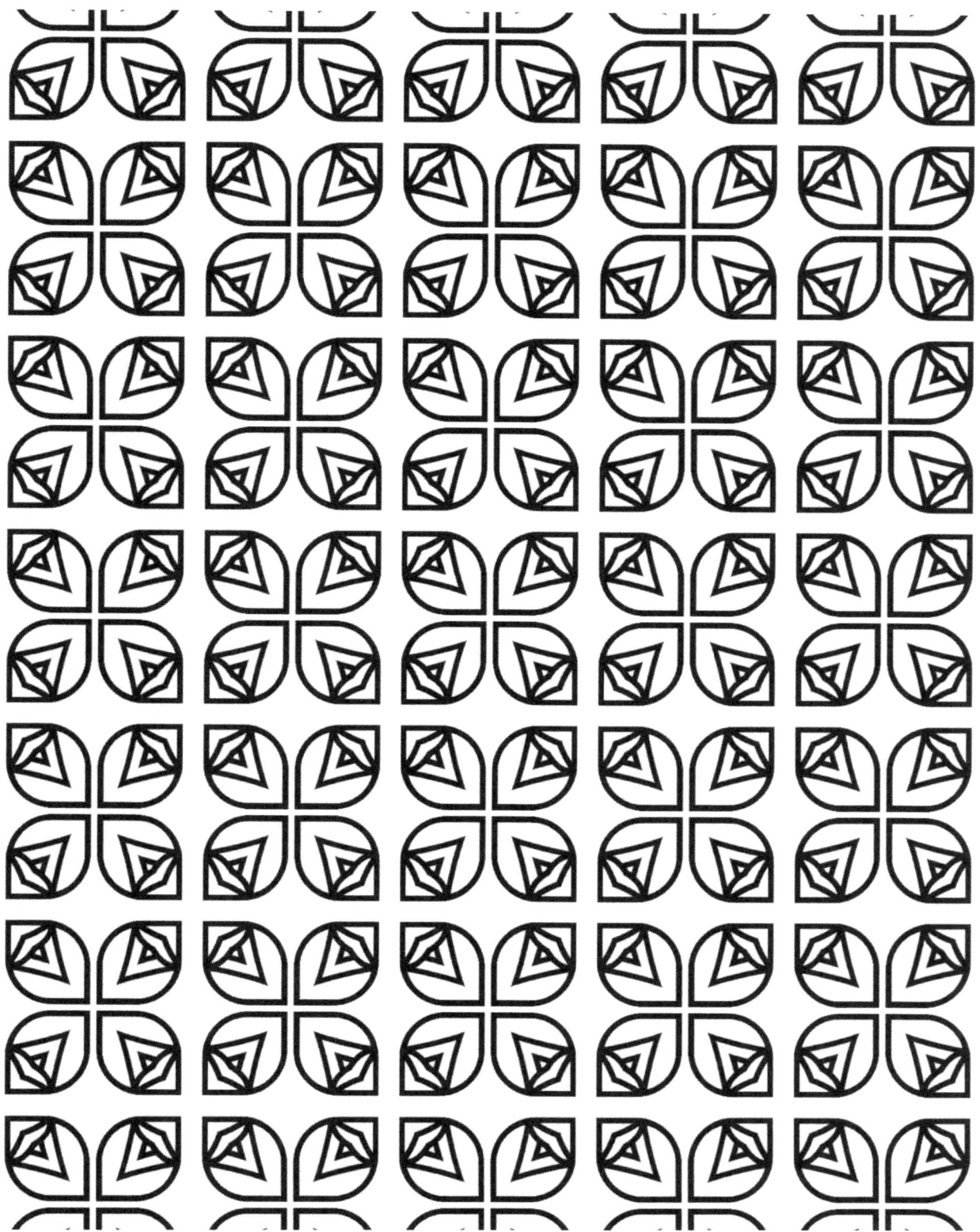

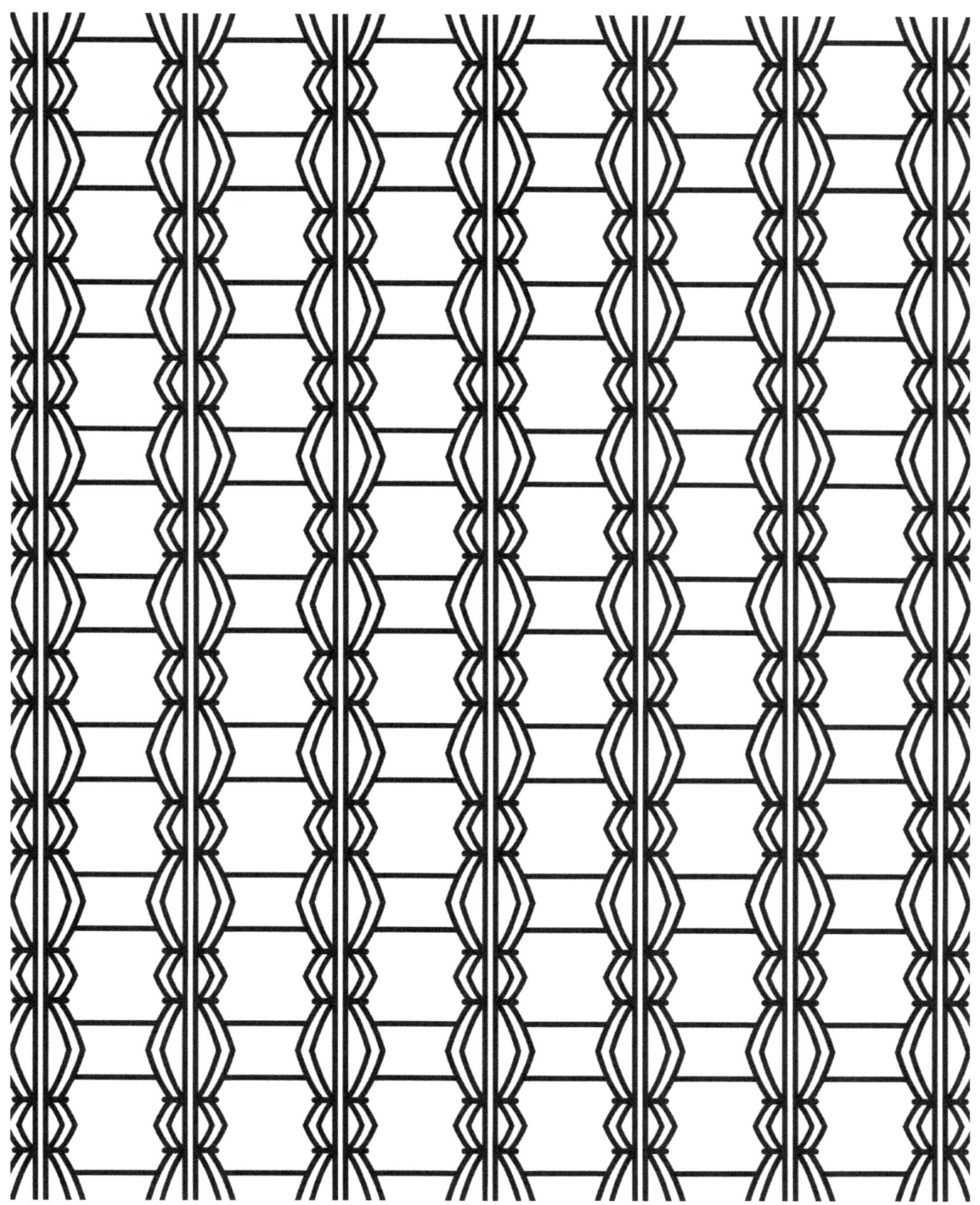

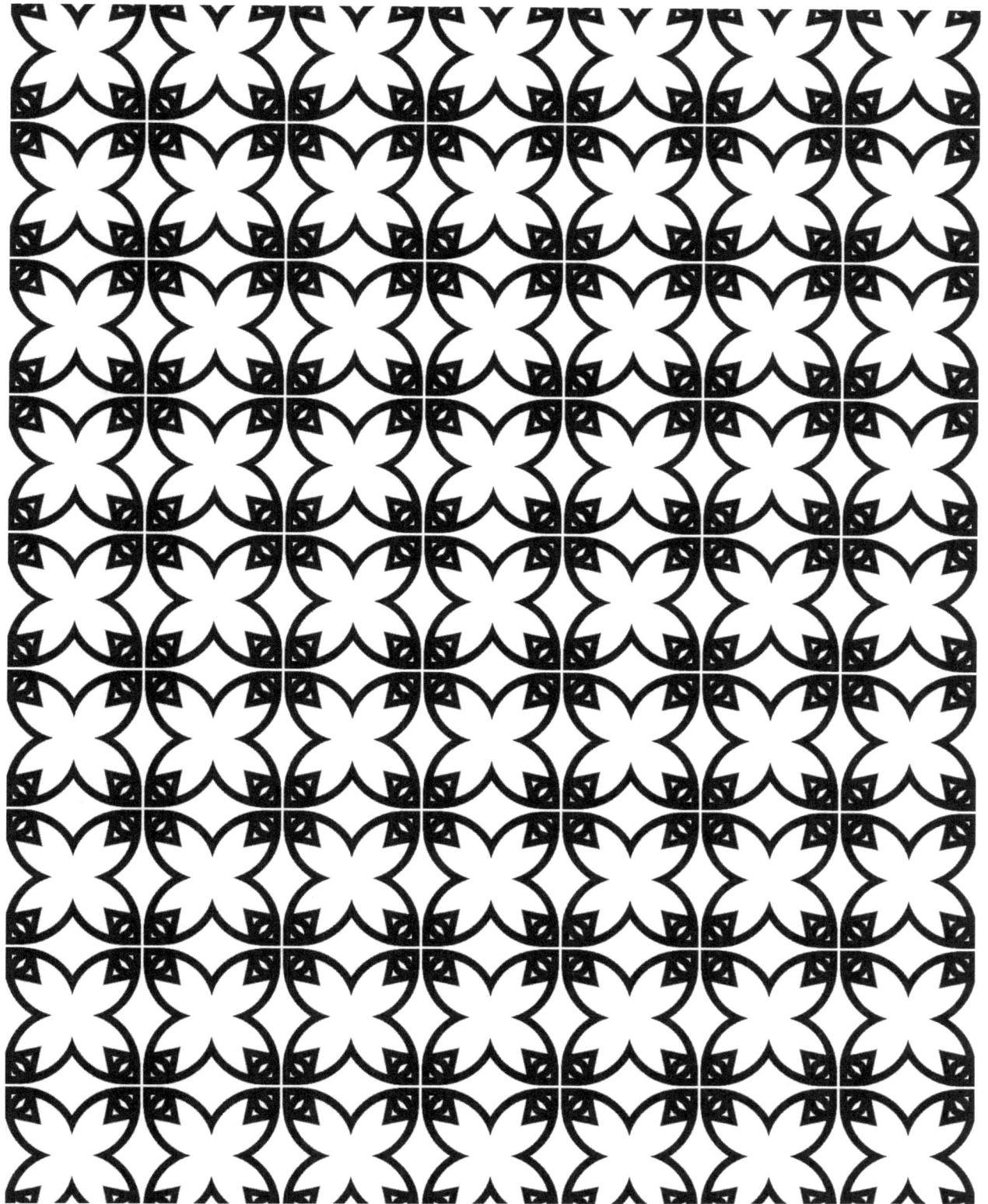

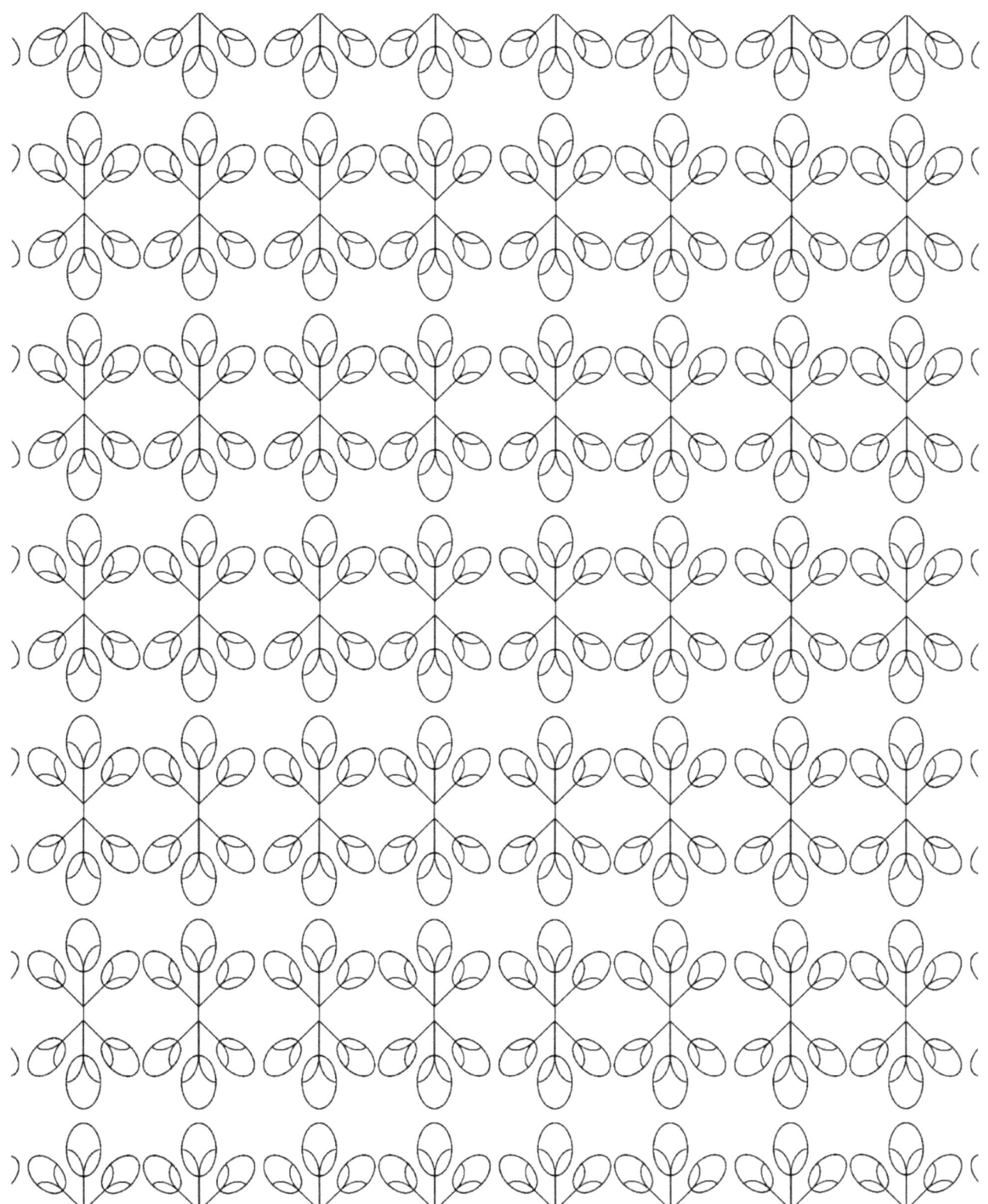

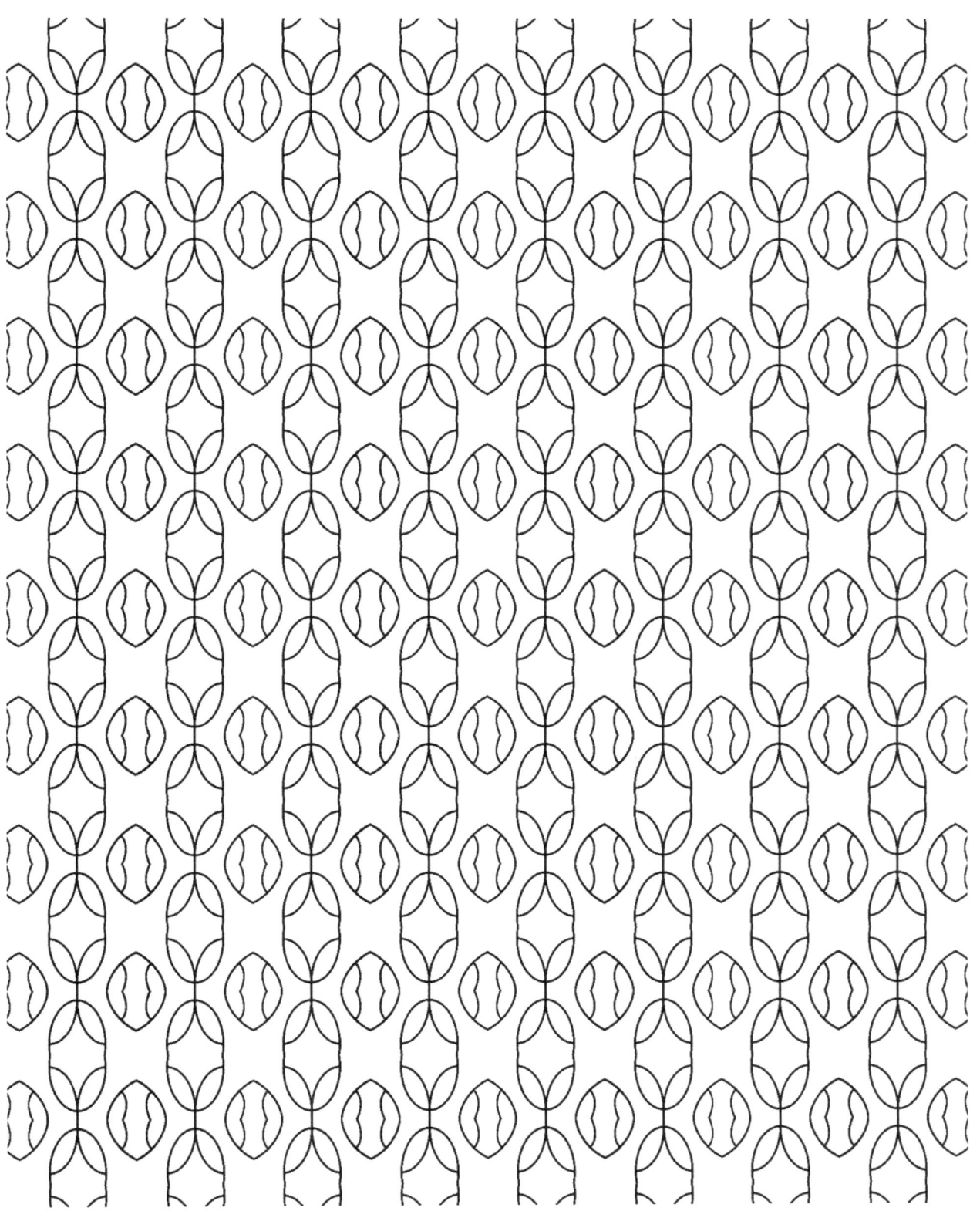

www.ingramcontent.com/pod-product-compliance
Lightning Source LLC
Chambersburg PA
CBHW081121180526
45170CB00008B/2955